Sorted
in 30 days
RELATIONSHIPS

To my wonderful husband Jim, with love and thanks

THIS IS A CARLTON BOOK

Text copyright © 2002 Caro Handley
Design and illustration copyright © 2002 Carlton Books Limited

This edition published by
Carlton Books Limited 2002
20 Mortimer Street
London W1T 3JW

A CIP catalogue record for this book
is available from the British Library
ISBN 1 84222 535 9

Printed and bound in Dubai

Editorial Manager:
Judith More
Art Director:
Penny Stock
Senior Art Editor:
Barbara Zuñiga
Executive Editor:
Zia Mattocks

Design:
Lewis Hallam
Editors:
Lisa Dyer and Libby Willis
Production Controller:
Janette Burgin
Illustrations:
Lucy Truman

Sorted
in 30 days

RELATIONSHIPS

how to keep your love alive
in just one month

caro handley

CARLTON
BOOKS

Contents

Introduction

Being in a relationship with someone you love is a truly wonderful thing. It's exciting, rewarding, enlightening and inspiring, but also hard work, challenging, painful and scary. Will it last? Can you really share your life, now and for ever, with this one person? Who doesn't ask herself those questions, no matter how good the relationship is? And when you are going through a rough patch, you may ask them about a hundred times a day.

Society sells us the fantasy that love will be a totally wondrous experience. We don't like to hear that love will involve pain as well as pleasure – that's what we learn as we go along. Sticking with a relationship, being committed and making it work are huge achievements. Courage is needed to hang on in there when the going gets tough, to learn from your mistakes and to carry on even when you're hurting. But it is more than worth it. To be in a loving relationship is to be blessed; it will bring deep happiness, benefit your health and enrich your life.

Follow this 30-day plan, and you will get the support and encouragement you need, tools for change, and greater resources and understanding to help you keep the love you've found and make the relationship the best it can be.

Day One

REAL LOVE

So you've found someone to love. Fabulous! Whether it's
been six days, six weeks, six years or longer, you want to
make it work and for this relationship to be the one that lasts
and grows stronger and better every day. That's why today, at
the very beginning, you need to take a look at what love is and what it means to you.
Love is discussed constantly and much has been written about it. But what is it? We
may see images of hearts and flowers, talk of romance and excitement, joy and
passion, but although love can include all these things, they don't explain what it is.

Some things love isn't
*   Chasing after someone who doesn't really want you.
*   Letting yourself be smothered, hurt or put down.
*   Trying to mould yourself into something you think you should be.
*   Always going along with what your partner wants.
*   Bouncing continually between highs and lows, excitement and tears.
*   Presenting only the 'acceptable' part of yourself to someone.
*   Drama, gossip, pretence or flattery.
*   Staying with someone to avoid being alone.
*   Shunning real closeness and intimacy.
*   Trying to fix someone or have them fix you.

If you are doing any of the above, it's time to stop and
review the relationship. This doesn't mean the relationship
has to end, but you may need to try to do some things
differently and see whether the relationship is strong enough
to survive the changes.

Some things love is

- Letting your partner know the real you, warts and all.
- Taking the time and trouble to get to know him, warts and all.
- Growing and learning together.
- Respecting one another.
- Developing trust between you.
- Staying committed even when you want to run away.
- Liking your partner.
- Sharing fears, doubts, hopes and dreams.
- Taking responsibility for yourself.
- Accepting what you don't like in your partner as well as what you do.

Think about the relationship. How many of the above are true for you and your partner? What strengths and weaknesses does the relationship have? Are there changes you need to make in yourself? What would you like to change about the way the two of you are together?

You may find that you are very clear on these points, which is a strong asset – you're already a step ahead. However, if you suspect things aren't quite right, but aren't sure why, don't worry; you will become clearer about any existing problems and what needs to be done about them as you work through the 30-day plan. Think of this day as the first step on an adventure, because that is what a relationship is – an adventure for two.

Be wise about love and choose the path to real love

Day Two

DREAMS

Look at the dreams you have for your relationship. We all have dreams, hopes and wishes that are precious and that we often keep secret from anyone else, fantasies of how things might be and of what we would love to happen. These dreams are important – we all need to believe that wonderful things are possible. And wonderful things can and do happen, but not without effort from us. We each need to make our own dreams come true.

Every relationship needs dreams because they create goals and give you and your partner a path to follow. Your dreams may be romantic, sensual, passionate and exciting. They may involve a big white wedding, setting up home in a country cottage with a picket fence, sailing around the world or raising a brood of children. Alternatively, your dreams may be more practical. Perhaps you imagine giving up your job, working with your partner to create your own business together or supporting your partner so that he can follow a dream of his own.

Take a long, hard look at your dreams. Do they focus around changes in your partner or in yourself? Do you dream that your partner will be kinder, more loving or more available? Do you dream of a time when you stop arguing or hurting each other?

Exercise

Take a pen and paper, and write down the dreams you have for your relationship. Imagine it is a year from now and then five years from now. What is the relationship like? What are you both doing, where do you live and how do you get along? Keep this as a record, adding to it as new wishes, hopes and dreams occur to you.

Over the next four weeks, begin making your dreams more possible and real. To do this, break them down into small steps and begin taking those steps, one by one. Even if your dreams seem a long way off or impossible, you can begin moving towards them. What would you need to do to make your dreams come true? What steps could you take, right now, to begin?

First, tell your partner about your dreams. Sharing is a little scary because it makes us feel vulnerable, but it is exciting, too, because it makes our dreams become more

real. Telling your partner will give him important information about you. Ask him to tell you about his dreams. Do you dream of the same things? Even if you don't, you can help and encourage one another so that some of your dreams do come true.

Think about other steps you can take. Do you need to open up more, to be braver about asking for what you want, to be firmer about saying no, or to work fewer hours, change jobs or start saving? Take the first step right now, and bring your dreams out of the shadows and into the open.

Make your dreams come true and keep love alive

Day Three

GROWING CLOSER

What does it mean to be close? Think about how close you and your partner are and look at ways of growing even closer. Intimacy is the basis of a good relationship, and it means being able to be open and to reveal your innermost thoughts to your partner without fear of being laughed at, criticized or rejected. To be really emotionally close to another person is wonderful because you can be yourself with them – no pretence, no effort, no cover-up – just you, as you are. To feel that you are loved and accepted for yourself means that you can relax, that you can make mistakes safe in the knowledge that they won't make any difference to the way you are loved.

We all have a 'shop front' that we present to the world, the part of us we think is attractive and acceptable. Then we have the 'back room', the stuff we keep hidden at first because we're not so proud of it. In an intimate relationship you can't keep the back room hidden, even if you try, and neither can your partner. Inevitably you are both going to show the sides of yourselves that you like the least – the aspects you fear will cause rejection or ridicule. When we are loved, instead of put down, we are fully accepted, and that's the best feeling in the world. But to be loved in this way you must be willing to let your partner know the real you.

How much have you let your partner know?

Answer yes or no to the following questions. Does your partner know:

- Your deepest fears and insecurities.
- The biggest hurts you've suffered in the past.
- The worst thing that's ever happened to you.
- What you are most ashamed of in your life.
- Who you love and who you hate.
- Your biggest embarrassment.
- How you really feel about your body.
- What you look like without any make-up in an old pair of pyjamas.
- The changes you would like to make to yourself.
- What you think your weaknesses and failings are.

How many times did you answer yes? This number will give you a clue about how intimate you are with your partner. If you answered yes fewer than seven times, you could allow your partner to come closer. Now ask yourself whether you know the answer to all these questions about your partner. How close does he let you come?

Make a decision today to allow your partner to come closer to the real you. To do this, simply be willing to open up and let him know more about you – the no-frills you. Offer information, talk about yourself and ask in return. Remember what your partner tells you and treat the information with respect. Let the relationship be a mutual journey of discovery.

Show the real you and grow closer every day

Day Four

BE HONEST

Let's look at honesty today, because if you want your partner to be honest then you must be honest, too. There are many ways of being dishonest in a relationship, including some which might not, at first, seem like dishonesty. But even subtle kinds attract problems and difficulties. Being honest can be hard at times and it can take a lot of courage, but the reward will be a healthy, strong relationship.

Ways in which we can be dishonest with our partner:

- You regularly flirt with someone else in a way you know would upset your partner; you tell yourself it's okay because your partner doesn't know about it.
- You fancy someone else and you've kissed; you tell yourself that you are not being unfaithful because you haven't had sex.
- You don't say what you really think in discussions with your partner.
- You don't express how you really feel about something important, such as sex, money or children.
- You lie about the past or about what you are up to now.
- You aren't straightforward about money matters.

Do you recognize any of the above? Are any true of you? Are there other ways in which, deep down, you know that you are not being truthful? If so, it's time to stop – today. When we are dishonest with others, it is impossible to feel really good about ourselves or to have a genuinely loving and happy relationship. Those things you have been untruthful about seem to grow bigger and more important as time goes on. You think of them more often and it can become exhausting. Invest in the relationship by telling the truth and behaving in an honest and open manner.

Being honest doesn't mean that you have to tell everything. If your partner is sensitive about past relationships, don't present a list of names and dates. There is always a place for discretion, and it is unnecessary to disclose something that will hurt your partner if it isn't relevant to the present. Honesty is about being authentic and truthful right now, about the issues that matter between you. It's about speaking up when it counts and trusting that you can find a way to sort out disagreements. It's about putting your partner and the relationship first, before anyone or anything else.

Be honest with your partner and yourself, and feel great

Day Five

RESPECT YOURSELF

Respect may sound like an old-fashioned word, but in any good relationship it matters enormously. Today's task is to consider just how much you respect yourself. If you treat yourself with respect, you are far more likely to be treated with respect by your partner. Other people respond to the signals we give them, so if you don't think well of yourself, others will sense it and respond accordingly. So what exactly does respect mean? It means treating yourself in a caring, considerate and decent way. Knowing your standards, sticking to them and believing that your opinions, thoughts and feelings have value.

Behaviour where self-respect is missing:

- You let your partner steamroller your opinions or feelings.
- You put up with being physically abused by your partner.
- You permit your partner to flirt even though this hurts you.
- You suspect your partner is unfaithful, but avoid taking steps to find out.
- You allow your partner to make all the decisions.
- You let your partner speak to you in an insulting or degrading way.
- You speak in an insulting way, or shout and scream when upset.
- You allow your partner to be rude to you in front of friends.
- You don't look after yourself by eating well, sleeping enough, getting exercise and caring for your body.
- You put yourself down in conversation.
- You tell yourself that you can't expect faithfulness/consideration/kindness because you're not worth it.
- You think your judgement is bad.

Do you recognize any of these? There are many other examples of lack of self-respect, but we usually know instinctively when it is missing. Lack of self-respect is about low self-esteem; when self-esteem is low, standards drop. Standards are vital in a relationship. You need to know what you think is right in order to judge whether something measures up to it or not. If you are behaving with a lack of self-respect, decide today to raise your self-esteem and standards, and to respect yourself – you will feel so much better when you do.

How to boost self-respect

- Never put up with any kind of bad treatment, such as violence, rudeness or unkindness. Make the message clear and, in extreme cases (especially violence), remove yourself from the situation until changes have occurred.
- Tell yourself that your feelings and opinions matter. Listen to them, trust them and follow them.
- Treat yourself in a loving, generous and considerate way.
- Make a list of standards you consider important, such as 'Violence is unacceptable', 'Being faithful is vital', and keep to them (see also Know Your Boundaries, page 52).

When you love and value yourself, you help others to treat you likewise, and you will find it easier to walk away from anyone who persists in treating you badly.

Treat yourself with respect and invite the respect of others

Day Six

RESPECT YOUR PARTNER

Just as it is vital to respect yourself, it is also very important to respect your partner. Love without mutual respect is sadly flawed. Take today to examine whether your behaviour towards your partner is respectful, considerate and kind.

In a long-term relationship, contempt can easily creep in. You may begin to take your partner for granted, to stop noticing those attributes that made you fall in love and to be aware only of the traits that irritate or annoy you. In doing this, you are focusing on the negative. There is a universal truth, which states, 'What you focus on grows'. When you concentrate on what you don't like, on your frustration, irritation or anxiety, it will grow. While focusing on the positive will increase the positive potential in the relationship.

Examples of treating your partner without respect:

- You make decisions without consultation.
- You plan your own life and expect him to fit in with it.
- You often criticize.
- You point out all the things he can't do.
- You put down or ridicule your partner in front of others.
- You forget anniversaries that are important to him.
- You are rude about your partner's family or friends.
- You are not interested in his feelings, wishes or needs.
- You are often impatient.
- You keep trying to make your partner change.

Are any of the above true of you? If even one is, you need to think about what is going on in the relationship. One partner is often stronger and more dominant than the other and may find it easy to lose respect for the partner who is slower, quieter, less dynamic, less confident or less outspoken. However, relationships need balance and most people need someone who is different from themselves in key ways. Learn to respect your partner for his qualities, talents and abilities. Perhaps he is slower and more reserved than you, but also more romantic and generous. Stop judging and believing that fast is better than slow, or that talking a lot is better than listening quietly.

Exercise

What are your partner's positive qualities? Remind yourself of the qualities that made you fall in love with him, then list them and start to notice them again. Recognize and write down the ways in which you balance one another.

Your partner deserves your best, not your worst. Many people treat strangers better than the person they love most. Imagine this scenario. A guest comes to dinner and spills a glass of wine on the carpet. What would you say? You would say it didn't matter, clear it up, bring another glass and try to make him or her feel at ease. If your partner spilled the wine, would you do the same? Or would you explode?

Begin to focus on the positive in your partner and the relationship. Bite your tongue when you feel a criticism coming and choose to say something appreciative instead. Speak warmly and treat your partner with love and respect. Remember that you are both equally important, valuable and special.

Respect your partner and the relationship will flourish

Day Seven

WHAT ABOUT ARGUMENTS?

All couples argue: some often, some rarely, most from time to time. Disagreements aren't necessarily a bad thing; in fact, many very happy couples have the occasional ferocious row and feel it's not a problem.

Be honest about the kind of arguments you generally have. 'Good' rows are underpinned by genuine liking and respect for one another. You can get issues off your chest but at the same time you both know where the boundaries lie. The row doesn't cause lasting hurt or carry on for hours. When one of you makes a 'peace move' – a word, gesture or look that says: 'Come on, let's stop' – the other responds by softening. Sometimes, however, arguments are a symptom of something wrong with the relationship.

When to worry about arguments:

- You end up simply swapping insults.
- The argument goes on for hours or even days.
- A serious row occurs every week or even more often.
- Hurtful things are said which you deeply regret.
- Language is cutting, cruel, critical or contemptuous.
- You ignore each other's attempts to defuse the argument.
- Walking away for half an hour doesn't cool you down.
- Violence, including slamming doors, throwing things and hitting or hurting yourself or the other person, is a feature of your arguments.

In a healthy argument, you may shout, argue and stomp around, but you do not get violent or blurt out things that you afterwards seriously regret. Criticism and contempt undermine any relationship; when these creep in, restoring goodwill, love and kindness becomes harder and harder.

If you are endlessly arguing about the same subject, look hard at it. Is it something that can't be resolved and which you will both have to learn to live with? If so, you need to agree to differ and deal with your own feelings about it in an adult way. Consider the following example. Your partner doesn't like your mother, but you want him to like her. This can't be resolved quickly, if at all, although when and how you see your mother can. Accept your partner's feelings, and deal with your own hurt and disappointment in an adult way, perhaps by talking to a friend, writing about it in a journal or booking a session with a counsellor.

Perhaps your regular argument is about something that can be resolved simply, such as who is responsible for certain household tasks or how to manage money. Choose a time when you are both in a good mood to sit down and sort out solutions (see also Negotiating Skills, page 25).

Make sure arguments are not damaging your relationship

Day Eight

LETTING GO

Today is the day to focus on cultivating a skill which will be enormously useful in creating a strong and happy relationship – the ability to let things go. Learning to walk away from conflict and to feel that whatever's at stake really doesn't matter too much will put your relationship on a firm foundation. It sounds simple, so why can't we do it all the time? In a conflict, we almost always have a big investment in being right. We are convinced that if we can only get the other person to see our point of view they will have to concede. The trouble is, they usually feel the same way, which leads to conflicts, arguments, discord and so on.

Exercise

Think of your last three arguments. Who was right? Do you believe it was you? Now ask your partner the same question; he will probably say it was actually him.

The solution to this apparently no-win situation is simply to let go of the need to be right. This becomes easier when you realize that there is seldom an absolute right and wrong, but only different points of view. If you asked a hundred people at random about your argument, half of them might agree with you and half might agree with your partner. Also remember that most conflicts seem unimportant a few hours or days later. So what if your partner had his hair cut too short (in your opinion) or if you packed too many clothes in the suitcase (in his opinion)? After all, it hardly matters in the great scheme of things.

Letting go

- When your partner upsets you, take a deep breath and count to ten. Or try to put some space between you for half an hour or so.
- Persuade yourself that this probably won't matter in a few days' time.
- If possible, look for a funny side to the argument – if you both start laughing, it will release the tension.
- Decide to be generous and let your partner be right. If you can say: 'Okay, you win, let's stop now,' he'll be so surprised that he may well decide you were right after all.
- Agree to postpone the argument while you both do something else. Reschedule it to a couple of hours later – chances are you'll no longer want to.

- Say: 'Let's both be right,' and hug.
- Tell yourself that people who are right all the time can be infuriating. Do you want to be one of them?
- Learn how to feel indignant without needing to start World War III. Let off steam in a hot bath, then reassess the issue when you feel calmer.
- Think about something wonderful – the best sex you ever had together, the holiday you are planning – to remind yourself how much you love each other.
- Tell yourself that if you win the argument, an hour later you will feel smug and self-satisfied – and miserable. And you probably won't be speaking to one another. But if you let it go, in an hour you'll be glad you did.

Learn to let things go and be a winner every time

Day Nine

NEGOTIATING SKILLS

Polish your negotiating skills today – they'll prove invaluable for your relationship. Many people think that negotiation is really about beating the other person into the ground, making him or her give in and getting your own way. This is actually more like bulldozing and doesn't leave anyone (even the winner) feeling good. Negotiation is about compromise, but it is also about creating a win-win situation in which you both come away feeling that you have made your point, gained something and felt good about yourself at the same time.

Although vital to living with and loving another person, negotiation is only possible if you believe that you are both entitled to a satisfying solution. Failing to negotiate leads to bitterness and resentment. The relationship will be out of balance and won't function well or be happy if things go all your way or all your partner's.

To begin, you must be willing to state your position, stand up for your rights and defend your case firmly but flexibly – which means giving up playing victim or persecutor. When you feel sorry for yourself, expect to be argued down or constantly give in, you are playing the role of the victim; when you steamroller your partner, behave aggressively or expect to come out on top every time, you become the persecutor. Neither of these roles is much fun either to play or to be around. Instead, choose to be adult and negotiate.

Guidelines for good negotiation

- Choose a time when you are both in a reasonably good mood.
  - Make sure that there won't be any interruptions, from children or telephone calls, for instance.
    - Sit at a table. This helps you feel more adult and businesslike, and ensures that you are both on the same level; avoid one person sitting and the other standing.
    - Take turns to put forward your case, making sure that you really LISTEN to one another.
- Be willing to concede some points.

- Know your bottom line, the limit beyond which you won't bargain.
- Put all possible solutions on the table.
- If the discussion gets heated, take a break and come back later.
- Search for a solution that you can both live with and which gives each of you part of what you want.
- If the solution doesn't work, be willing to come back to the table and try to find a different one.

Of course, there will always be non-negotiable points, and you have to decide what these are. However, negotiating on more flexible or less clear-cut issues (and most things can be seen in shades of grey, rather than black and white) can prove mutually rewarding and revealing.

Choose to believe that a solution can always be found

Day Ten

SORT OUT SEX

Good sex is part of a good relationship. To be lovers as well as friends, you need sex, and if the sex is going wrong the rest of the relationship will suffer, too. Sex is an important ingredient of romantic love, so it's worth devoting time and effort to it.

Exercise

How would you rate your sex life, on a scale from 1 to 10? If it's 8 or above, that's great – think of today as a refresher course. Any lower, though, and there is definite room for improvement.

First, identify what's going wrong. Here are some common symptoms of a less-than-satisfactory sex life:

- You are not satisfied, you don't have orgasms, or you have orgasms but not much fun before or after them.
- Sex is always the same old routine, and you are bored.
- Your partner doesn't really know how to turn you on.
- You are not attracted to your partner, or you feel he isn't attracted to you.
- One of you is too tired – or you both are.
- Children always seem to interrupt.
- You've never really enjoyed sex.
- There's always too much on your mind.
- There are some things you don't like doing in bed, which upsets your partner so that you both become tense.

Do any of these scenarios sound familiar? If so, don't worry: sex often proves an easy area to improve. If you have had good sex in the past, you know how marvellous it can be, and it's just a question of rediscovering it. And if sex has never been great for the two of you, now's the time to make it so. Loving and caring for each other will enable you to have great sex. In fact, the more relaxed and familiar you are with one another, the better the sex can be. Sex can become boring with time – if you let it – but it can also get better and better . . .

How to have great sex

Get the scene right

Agree not to argue or discuss big issues in the bedroom – keep talk warm and loving there. Make the room a beautiful place to be, with soft sheets, candles, scents and so on.

Enjoy the build-up

Bathing together is nice and making love to someone who is fresh and clean is even nicer. Watch a sexy video (not porn, just a bit of lust) if you like, or a funny movie, because laughing relaxes you and makes you feel happy.

Put worries, stress and children beyond the bedroom door

And don't let them in – use a lock on the door if possible.

Start slowly

Try massaging, stroking or kissing each other all over. Sooo sexy …

Think sexy and you'll feel sexy

The sexiest part of you is your brain, so use fantasies of the best sex you've ever had or of making love in outrageous places to stimulate your body's responses.

Talk

Tell your partner how sexy he is, how much you fancy him and how much you like what he's doing (when you do). In return, ask what he enjoys – and do it.

Experiment

Without doing anything that makes you feel uncomfortable, explore new territory, such as role-playing or different positions.

Ignore tiredness

Once you make the effort, sex can actually restore your energy if you are tired, and it will help you sleep better afterwards!

Decide today to make your sex life the best it can be and to think of your partner as the sexiest person in the world, now and for ever.

Great sex can be a wonderful part of a great relationship

Day Eleven

KEEP THE LAUGHTER FLOWING

Never forget the power of laughter: relationships run more smoothly and happily with a hefty dose of humour thrown in. Laughter works like magic. The simple act of moving your facial muscles into a smile or a laugh, even if you don't feel like doing it, has an astonishing effect. It causes your brain to release 'feel good' hormones, which then flood your body, making you feel better, lighter and happier.

Exercise

Try this today. Smile at everyone you meet. Not only will it make you feel better, but you will also receive a warmer response from others.

In a relationship, laughter can break a deadlock, lighten a grim mood, stop an argument and improve sex. Laughter heals hurts and brings you closer. The more you laugh, the more you lighten up, and that's good for all aspects of life. If either of you is a worrier or prone to anxiety, laughing can help alleviate the stresses.

How to bring more laughter into your life
- Go to a comedy club or watch comedy programmes on television.
- Read a humorous novel.
- Tickle each other (if you both like it).
- Share any good jokes you have heard.
- Remember and relate funny stories you heard or read, or experiences you had during the day.
- Keep videos that made you laugh and play them when you need a lift.
- Be willing to see the funny side of anything, especially sex.

Often the lighter side of life is overshadowed when couples settle down together. Suddenly bills, children and responsibilities swamp them and laughter evaporates. Little children laugh dozens of times a day. Be more like them and find a lot to laugh about. Be playful with one another, too. Have pillow fights, chase each other in the park, fool around when you have the chance. Everyone loves to be around people who take life lightly. Taking life lightly means knowing that whatever happens isn't the end of the world; it means keeping perspective and trusting that it will all come right. Life should never be so serious that there's no room for laughter.

For a happy, harmonious relationship, keep laughing

Day Twelve

ANGER

Think about the role of anger in your relationship. Everyone gets angry from time to time, and we each deal with it in different ways. Many people feel uncomfortable with their anger, or other people's, and it may bring up deep-seated fears and tensions. Perhaps you weren't allowed to be angry when you were a child because your parents disapproved of displays of anger and you learnt to hide it. But hiding anger doesn't make it disappear – it just leaks out in other ways.

How do you deal with anger?

- You pretend you aren't angry, suppressing it, but end up exploding later.
- You hold it in and become ill as a result.
- You turn anger into resentment and walk around feeling like a martyr.
- You let it leak out gradually in bursts of criticism and irritation.
- You wait until anger has built up to the point where you shout and scream.

Do any of the above responses sound familiar? Almost all of us do one or more of the above at some point, and many of us do them often. But dealing with anger in these ways is not much fun and can be very destructive, so make the decision today to try a different approach.

Coping with anger in positive ways

Tell yourself that it's okay to be angry

Anger is just a feeling, like any other, and you can't stop yourself feeling angry any more than you can stop yourself feeling lonely or sad. The important thing is how you BEHAVE when you feel angry.

Don't behave badly when you are angry

If you do, you will make yourself miserable. Choose not to shout, scream, sulk, carp, criticize or slam doors.

Do something constructive

Sometimes it's enough simply to acknowledge your anger, telling yourself, 'I'm really angry about . . .'. You could also try the following: shut yourself in the car and scream; write an angry letter but don't send it; write in a journal; punch a pillow; or exercise.

Anger can be a sign that something needs to change

If this is the case, identify what it is and begin taking steps to change it.

Remember that feelings follow behaviour

When you change your actions, your mood will follow. Sometimes the fastest way out of an angry frame of mind is to alter your behaviour. Go for a walk, dance, do anything you find fun, and your anger will subside.

Express your anger appropriately

Sometimes you need your partner to know that you are angry and to act differently. Try this approach: simply and clearly state why you are angry, tell your partner how the behaviour makes you feel, then say exactly what you would like your partner to do.

To defuse potentially explosive situations, always be specific, rather than general, and avoid insults. Use 'I' statements rather than 'you' statements. For example, don't say: 'You always attack me in front of my friends, you're a nasty, thoughtless creep.' Do say: 'I was really hurt tonight when you made that comment in front of our friends. I'd like you to treat me with respect and talk to me politely.' Your partner is then far more likely to listen and do what you want.

Let go of your fears, and use anger as a tool for positive change

Day Thirteen

FRIENDS

When we begin a committed relationship, there is always some adjusting to do in our friendships. Sometimes friends welcome the relationship, but sometimes they don't; they may willingly take a back seat, or they may not. Friends are precious, and keeping them when you enter into a romantic relationship is important, but it's equally important not to let them dominate or sabotage the relationship. A careful balance needs to be reached between your partner and your friends.

Are your friends more important to you than your partner? Are they intruding into relationship territory? Here are some warning signs:

- You regularly ask your best friend for advice about the relationship, then follow it.
- You discuss intimate details of the relationship with a friend, things you know your partner would be uncomfortable about you divulging.
- You prefer an evening with a friend to an evening with your partner.
- You often cancel plans with your partner because a friend has a problem (however minor) and wants advice.

If any of the above ring true for you, listen to the warning bells: three in a relationship doesn't work. A friend this closely involved is almost certain to be undermining your relationship. Friends like this are seldom supportive of the relationship; they may be jealous and want you all to themselves.

Getting the balance right

Remember that your partner comes first. He or she needs to be the person who matters most in your life. The two of you are a unit, and the people around you need to know that they can't possibly divide you.

Keep friendships within clear boundaries. Friends don't come on dates with the two of you and don't take priority over your arrangements with your partner, unless there is a genuine crisis.

Stop discussing the more intimate aspects of the relationship with your friends. Some things between you and your partner should stay private – instinct will tell you what these are.

The balance, though not always easy to achieve, is crucial. Friends need to know that they matter to you and that you will be there for them, but at the same time make it clear to everyone that your partner comes first. Always remember that a true friend will respect and encourage a relationship that makes you happy and will gladly step back to make room for your partner.

There is room in your life for both your partner and friends

Day Fourteen

FAMILY

Today, after friends, it's time to look at the role of family – yours and your partner's – in the relationship. Some of the advice on friendships (see page 34) also applies to family, but there are other more complex and subtle ways in which families can interfere in relationships. Be on the lookout for these and nip them in the bud. No matter how precious your mother, father, sister or brother, they are not the person who will live with you, share decisions and choices, and shape a life together. They have their own lives and need to take a back seat in yours. Your family may be deeply important to you, but your relationship is most important of all – it is about your future.

How families, especially parents, can undermine the relationship:

- Criticizing your partner in subtle, or not so subtle, ways.
- Giving constant advice on how to run your relationship, home, life and so on.
- Offering money to you or your partner in a way that upsets the balance of the relationship.
- Demanding an impossible degree of attention.
- Bribing you (or your partner) to leave the relationship; for example, by promising an inheritance.
- Competing with you; for example, it is not uncommon for a man's mother to compete with his new partner.
- Bullying.
- Insisting that the relationship won't last.

If any of the above are threatening your relationship, it's time to take action. Be absolutely sure that the role of family members is to be supportive and encouraging, offering help or advice with sensitivity or only when asked. Be firm about setting boundaries and resisting their interference. This can be done without causing dramas or estrangement. Simply smile and say: 'Thank you, but no,' or brush criticism aside, while making it clear that your relationship is solid and strong.

Interfering relatives can, and often do, destroy a relationship. Of course, there are times when parents or family members have genuine concerns about a specific problem. If this is the case, thank them for their concern and decide for yourself what action to take.

Always remember that the relationship is your decision. You don't need anyone else's permission or approval for your choice of partner. If the relationship is right for you, that's all that matters. As an adult you get to celebrate your own successes and deal with your problems and mistakes.

Make it clear to family members that your relationship comes first

Day Fifteen

TRUST

To have a successful relationship you need to be able to trust one another, and to trust one another, you need to behave in a way that is trustworthy. Trust without foundation only leads to hurt and disillusion. Trusting someone the minute you meet him, though you may have a strong instinct that he is trustworthy and want to follow it, is inappropriate. Even if you feel this way, go slowly. Wait until you know that the person is truly as trustworthy as you hoped he would be before you invest your trust in him.

Many people trust too soon and get hurt. Others stay suspicious and refuse to trust, even when they are with someone who is clearly worthy of trust. When this happens, they are bringing their lack of trust from the past into the present.

How do you know whether someone is worthy of trust?
Here are some signs to look for:

Does your partner do what he says he will do?
This is the most important indicator of trustworthiness. You have a right to expect someone who says he will phone on a certain day or at a certain time to keep his word. The same applies to everything else your partner says he will do.

If your partner is always too ready with excuses, be warned
Unreliability is immature, selfish and often a sign of deeper untrustworthiness.

Does your partner have secrets?
If he won't tell you things about himself, or behaves in a secretive way, ask yourself what he might want to hide.

Behaving in a trustworthy way yourself is important. You can't expect to attract someone worth trusting unless you are worth trusting, too. Make sure that you act in an open, honest, consistent, reliable and fair way.

If you believe that your partner is behaving in an untrustworthy way, you must decide whether you will accept this or not. Explain your worries and fears, and don't invest trust until you know that this is the right thing to do. However, be alert to the danger of being overly suspicious. If you are refusing to trust someone who is behaving in a clear and open way, then you need to make changes. Recognize that your doubts belong in the past, with some other situation or person. Perhaps someone else – a parent, for instance – abandoned you and now your fear of abandonment is holding the relationship back. Look at your partner with fresh eyes and be willing to trust where trust has been earned.

Always behave in a way that is worthy of trust

Day Sixteen

APPRECIATION

So often we begin a relationship full of appreciation, noticing the little things a lover does for us and loving everything about him. Then, all too soon, we get used to one another, the special things become ordinary and appreciation is lost. Today, remind yourself of all there is to appreciate in your partner and the relationship.

Appreciation is about making people feel good about themselves, counting your blessings and focusing on all that is good. Sometimes we notice and appreciate, but we don't say anything. Voicing your appreciation and letting your partner know what you value and appreciate about him is always a good move in a relationship. If you notice, and comment on, the ways in which your partner is kind, generous, brave, supportive and encouraging, the qualities you love about him, he will feel cherished. Learning to appreciate can also help you find the good in any situation and turn potentially difficult or unhappy situations around.

Exercise 1

Take a pen and paper, and list ten things you appreciate about your partner. Have fun with the list, adding more as you think of them. You might include:

- Qualities, such as generosity, loyalty, courage or humour.
- Talents, such as being a great lover or cook.
- Developed skills, such as rock-climbing or an advanced degree.
- Commitment to the relationship.
- How he takes responsibility for aspects of his life.
- Hard work.
- Dress sense.
- Appearance or voice.
- Sensitivity in difficult situations.
- Willingness to support you, emotionally and/or financially.

Exercise 2

Now make a second list of qualities that you appreciate about yourself, because this is just as important as appreciating your partner.

Exercise 3

Make a third list of aspects of the relationship and the way the two of you are together that you appreciate, adding to them as they occur to you. You might include:

- The way you have stuck together through problems and rough patches.
- How you both deal with arguments and find resolutions.
- The laughter and fun in the relationship.
- Your ability to balance being together with the other demands in life.
- Romantic gestures you make to one another.
- The way you put one another first.
- Mutual contributions to running the home.
- Willingness to be flexible about decisions.
- Responsibilities each of you take in your joint life.
- The support you give one another in doing what matters to each of you.

As you write the lists you will be surprised by how much you are grateful for. Make appreciation a habit from now on. Every day, find three things to admire about your partner and make sure you communicate them.

Appreciation is the key to goodwill and happiness

Day Seventeen

MONEY MATTERS

All too often, money becomes a problem between a couple and a major source of arguments and tensions, and this isn't surprising. When you enter a relationship, you each take all kinds of money issues and attitudes with you. One partner's point of view can be very different to the other's. A compromise has to be found and common ground negotiated, and for this you need plenty of tolerance and goodwill.

Examples of different attitudes to money:

- One of you thinks the other spends far too much, or thinks the other person is mean.
- One partner earns more and resents being the major breadwinner.
- One partner earns much less and feels inferior or resents being dependent.
- One of you hates figures and leaves the other to take charge of the accounting.
- One of you thinks all will work out in the end, while the other worries and frets.
- Priorities can't be agreed between the two of you; for example, you want a mortgage, but your partner wants extra holidays, or he wants to save while you want to eat out more often.

The answer to all these problems – and any others that you have identified – is a blend of compromise, understanding and negotiation.

How to solve money issues

- No matter who earns the most, you should both have an equal say about joint spending issues. The bigger earner doesn't have more clout in this case.
- Agree from the start to listen to and respect one another's point of view.
- Sit down, in peace and quiet, and in a good mood, and put all the money issues and decisions on the table.
- Go through each issue one by one, taking turns to have your say. Look for areas of compromise. For example, could you save a little more and still go out to dinner reasonably often? Could you opt for a smaller mortgage and manage one extra holiday (perhaps a weekend break) each year?
- Agree who is in charge of book-keeping and plan to meet regularly – weekly or monthly – to keep up to date on finances and make decisions for the future.

- Make sure that you both have your own money, as well as a joint fund. Ideally, keep separate accounts, plus a joint account for household expenses.
- Agree that neither of you can comment on how the other chooses to spend personal money. Only the money in the joint account is up for negotiation.

The key to resolving money tensions is to keep everything open, uncomplicated and clear. Be willing to find a compromise to any problem, however insoluble it seems.

Don't let money come between you – ever

Day Eighteen

LOOK AFTER YOURSELF

Today you need to focus on the way you look after yourself in the relationship. Women, especially, often concentrate all their energies on their partners, but of course this can happen the other way around, too. When all your attention and energy is expended on the other person, you neglect your own needs and desires. What happens then is almost always bad for both of you.

Just as you are trying to meet your partner's needs and give him everything he wants, so you expect your partner to look after you and give you what you want. This can be a recipe for disaster. As you discover your needs aren't being met, you get whiny, resentful and needy, which makes you steadily less attractive. Your partner, feeling under pressure, wants to run a mile. In fact, the pressure on your partner is doubled: he has you trying to please him, which can feel like a big burden, and then has the added pressure of being expected to look after you. In your efforts to please your partner, you are actually making him (and yourself) miserable.

If this is happening in your relationship, be honest and recognize that it's time to stop. This scenario can break a relationship very quickly, and that's sad because there is no need for it.

Breaking the needy/pleasing cycle

Start developing your 'selfish' muscle. Being selfish can be a good thing because it means learning to look after your own needs and wants without expecting someone else to fulfil them for you.

Sit down, right now, with a pen and paper and ask yourself: 'What do I want?'. List ten things you want which you would normally do without or hope that your partner would provide. For instance, you might want to have time to read or paint; to have a cup of tea in bed in the morning, a foot massage or a special dinner; or to redecorate the home. Getting the hang of working out what you want can take a while, so add to the list as you think of more.

How many things on the list could you provide for yourself? Probably all of them. Begin right now, today, with something you can do for yourself. Make this a habit: every time you feel grumpy, critical or sorry for yourself, think about something that you really want and either give it to yourself or plan to as soon as possible.

Stop doing everything for your partner. Give up trying to anticipate what your partner wants or trying to fix things for him. Stand back and let him sort things out for himself.

Behave towards one another in a caring way, but don't overdo it or caring can become smothering and overwhelming. The antidote to smothering behaviour is to keep bringing the spotlight back to you. The more you put the spotlight on your own needs, the less you will put it on your partner's. Every time you are tempted to fuss and do something for your partner which he doesn't really need you to do, do something for yourself instead. A huge amount of pressure on the relationship will be eased and you will be a lot more fun to be around.

Look after yourself as well, and your relationship will thrive

Day Nineteen

ASK FOR WHAT YOU WANT

After learning to look after yourself, the next step forward is to learn to ask for what you want. So many relationships would be much easier if couples would only ask rather than expect the other to guess. What you think is obvious (that you want a hug, for example) probably isn't obvious at all. So when your partner does what he thinks you want instead (perhaps leaving you alone instead of hugging you), you feel upset and angry. Your partner can't understand what he did wrong and the spiral of disappointment continues. Wouldn't it have been so much simpler if you had just asked for a hug in the first place?

Why don't most of us ask for what we want? Here are some of the reasons:

- We don't know what we want so we can't ask for it.
- We're afraid we won't get it.
- We think we don't deserve it.
- We think we've got to earn it by pleasing the other person first.
- We think it won't be special if we've had to ask for it.

Do any of these apply to you? Very few people know how to ask for what they want, regularly, and feel good about it. Most of us have a big resistance to asking. But just like any other kind of behaviour, requesting what you want is a habit you can cultivate, simply by being willing to do it over and over again until it feels easy and familiar.

How to ask for what you want

- Remember that people who love you are usually more than willing to give you what you want, if they can.
- Consider some of the things you want – chances are they are really quite simple.
- Practise asking in a direct but warm way. Avoid whining, pleading, cajoling or flattering.
- Be willing to settle for SOME of what you want. Abandon the idea that you have to have it all.
- Remember that it's a real relief for the other person when you say what you want. He can stop guessing, and this saves a lot of energy and grief.
- If your partner says no, accept that the answer is not a rejection of you, but that they simply can't do it, for his own reasons.
- Learn how to receive graciously. When you do get what you want, show him how appreciative you are and then enjoy it. Don't use it as an excuse to trigger off a guilt trip or decide you have to give your partner double what he has just given you.

Sometimes receiving can be a lot harder than giving, so remind yourself that you deserve it and relax. Once you both get the hang of it, asking for what you want can bring you closer – so go on, give it a try.

Be brave and generous, and ask for what you want

Day Twenty

ALWAYS BE YOU

Too often, in a relationship, we lose track of who we are. We are so busy focusing on the other person or on being part of a couple that suddenly we can't find our own identity. A successful relationship is not about being half of a whole, but about two wholes coming together in harmony. So it's important to keep your individual identity strong and not to feel that something of the essential you has been lost or smothered.

Signs of loss of identity:

- You can't make decisions about anything, even which film you'd like to see, without consulting your partner.
- You feel weird going to social events on your own.
- You never arrange to do things without him if you can help it.
- You always shop together.
- If your partner is away for a night, you panic.
- You don't enjoy your own company.
- You've stopped doing things that you used to enjoy because your partner doesn't want to do them.
- You would rather be with him than without him, even if it means going to an event or joining in an activity you don't like.
- You use the word 'we' more often than the word 'I'.
- You can't imagine life without your partner; if he died, you'd have to die, too.

Do any of these ring true? Are you so immersed in coupledom that the mere thought of being just 'me' or 'I' makes you feel afraid and lonely? If so, it's time to stop subsuming your identity in your partner's. You can learn to stand on your own two feet without losing the closeness you share.

Being yourself while staying in love

Nurture friendships that are just yours. Make dates to see your friends regularly, without your partner.

Set aside time to do what you enjoy. Spend at least one night a week on an activity that you enjoy – yoga, photography, or going to see a movie with friends – and which doesn't involve your partner.

Exercise your decision-making and opinion 'muscles'. Frequently ask yourself: 'What do I think about this?', 'What would I like to do now' or 'What kind of evening out would suit me?' This doesn't mean you always have to have your way, but helps you to know what you think and want.

Make sure that there are times when you don't think or talk about your partner. Don't go out with friends and then talk only about your partner; instead, discuss life, politics, fashion, books, music – anything that helps you branch out.

Don't automatically do everything with him. If you bathe together too often, it may stop being special. Keep the buzz by rationing some of the things you do together so that they remain special rather than routine.

Don't do what your partner wants to do just to be with him. If asked to go along to a football match or a yoga class, don't trail along if you don't actually enjoy it. Do something you like instead.

Keep your life interesting and it will keep you interesting, too. Make sure that you always have enough to talk about and that you do some things on your own. Never take togetherness too far.

Always believe that if you lost your partner, you would be strong enough to go on with a fulfilling, enriching life. No couples know how long they have together, but believing that you would cope alone will make you happier and stronger now.

Be yourself and stay whole and happy

Day Twenty-One

KNOW YOUR BOUNDARIES

A boundary is like a limit: it is a line that should not be crossed, a point which is as far as you can comfortably go. In relationships, just as in life, we need boundaries. They help us feel safe, comfortable and whole, and they define who we are. Boundaries are neither good nor bad. Everyone's are different and we choose them simply because they feel right for us. Whether we are aware of them or not, we all have them. However, many of us have weak or absent boundaries in certain areas, and this can lead to feelings of being easily overwhelmed and stressed.

Signs of weak or missing boundaries

You decide on an activity, but then change your mind because your partner asks you to do something else. You are planning a night in, reading a good book, until your partner asks you to go out; you don't want to go, but you do anyway.

You make a mutual rule or promise, but then break it or ignore your partner breaking it. You decide not to take telephone calls after midnight. You tell your partner, then answer the telephone as usual when a friend calls at 1 am a few days later. Or, you promise to stop smoking, but then carry on.

You decide that certain behaviour is unacceptable, but then accept it. You tell your partner that you will leave if he hits you, then stay after you've been hit again.

Exercise

Try to define your boundaries, establishing new ones if you need them, then make a promise to keep them in place. You don't need hundreds – too many can be as bad as too few – but the ones you do put in place must be the right and important ones for you.

When fixing boundaries, remember a couple of points. Firstly, other people will always test your boundaries. If you hold the line, they will respect you and know that you mean what you say; if you don't, they will know you're a pushover. Secondly, be prepared to stick to your boundaries; don't make one you know you're going to break, as you will feel that you can't trust yourself.

For these two reasons, choose boundaries that are important enough to keep. For example, pick an issue that has been bothering you and decide where the boundary needs to be. You will soon discover how good it feels to stick to your decision, even when your partner tests you by trying to break it.

**Keep your boundaries and trust yourself
to mean what you say**

Day Twenty-Two

RESPONSIBILITY

To keep love strong, both partners in a relationship need to be responsible. If your reaction to this is, 'How boring, that sounds dull and worthy,' think again. Being responsible doesn't just mean paying your bills and buying the groceries – it runs far deeper than that.

True love entails being willing to take responsibility. This means acting in a consistent and appropriate way, and when we do this we create deep and meaningful bonds. Few things kill love faster than a total lack of responsibility on the part of either partner; if you have ever been affected by this, you will know how true it is. Those who behave irresponsibly are willing to let others down, to burden others, to use others as cover, to create problems and to cause hurt. There is no place for any of this in a strong and healthy relationship. Take a look at your relationship. Are you being irresponsible or putting up with your partner's irresponsible behaviour?

Strengthening your levels of responsibility

Always behave in a way of which you can be proud. Identify areas of behaviour that cause you shame and clean them up.

Remember that love and responsibility go together. You can't claim to love someone without being willing to behave responsibly towards them.

Responsibility begins with yourself. Are you looking after and nurturing yourself? Are you getting enough rest, good food and exercise? You won't be able to respond appropriately to the demands of life and your relationship unless you are fulfilling the basic responsibilities to yourself.

Behaving responsibly towards your partner means doing what you've said you'll do and keeping your half of any agreements made. It doesn't mean fussing, fixing or smothering your partner. Sometimes the responsible act is to step back and let him sort out his own mess.

When deciding what your responsibilities are, the key word is 'appropriate'. Use this as a measure to ensure that you don't overdo it.

If the irresponsible person is your partner

Let your partner feel the consequences of his actions. In other words, don't always cover up for him, rescue him from fixes of his own making or do something that he really should do for himself. Stand back and let him deal with whatever happens.

Make your own boundaries clear. Let your partner know what you will and won't do and what you expect from him. Don't drone on – just say it once, then leave it.

Decide whether you really want to be around someone who is consistently irresponsible. You may want to withdraw, partially or wholly, rather than live with behaviour that causes problems for you.

If the irresponsibility is just in specific areas, tackle them by making the consequences clear. For example, if your partner always arrives very late to meet you, let him know that you will wait ten minutes before leaving.

Tackling irresponsibility is an exciting challenge. It means being willing to stand up and be counted, to set your boundaries and to acknowledge the powerful connection between responsibility and love.

Be responsible and feel good about who you are

Day Twenty-Three

THE GREEN-EYED MONSTER

Jealousy is undermining and destructive. Everyone is jealous from time to time, but consistent jealousy causes deep rifts in a relationship. Today is the day to examine the role jealousy plays in your relationship. Are you or your partner consistently jealous? Is jealousy an issue between you? If so, it's time to do something about it.

If either of you is experiencing feelings of jealousy, ask yourself: 'Is there a reason?' Is one of you causing it by behaving inappropriately? Sometimes all the blame is laid on the partner who is jealous when the other partner has played a part in the problem. Are you both behaving in a trustworthy and appropriate way (see Trust, page 38)? Are you putting your partner first, not flirting or spending too much time with other people, and treating one another with care, respect and consideration? Tackle these areas and the jealousy should disappear. If jealousy continues to be a problem, the root cause may be insecurity and low self-esteem (see also Respect Yourself, page 16).

How to deal with your jealousy
Begin to build up your self-esteem and sense of self-worth
The stronger these are, the less jealous you will be. Talk to yourself in positive ways, appreciate all the good in what you are and what you do and be kind to yourself.

Talk to your partner about the problem
Ask for his support in dealing with it and discuss particular triggers for your jealousy – your partner may be able to offer help at these times.

List all the reasons why you are loved
Reassure yourself that you are lovable, worthwhile and worthy of your partner.

Make the decision to stop being jealous
Refuse to let anything be bigger than you or beyond your control – the relationship is too precious to damage or lose.

When you feel jealousy rising, do something different
Focus on times when you've felt great about yourself and, if need be, remove yourself from the situation until the jealousy has gone.

Tackling jealousy in these ways, firmly and consistently, will enable you to control it. If your partner is jealous, offer to support him in every reasonable and appropriate way, as long as he is willing to deal with his feelings, too. Encourage your partner to feel good about himself and to feel loved. Often jealousy is a passing phase. Plenty of couples have found it a problem at some stage, but have dealt with it successfully, so take heart.

Don't let jealousy damage the love between you

Day Twenty-Four

SLOW AND SURE

Today, focus on the importance of taking your time in all things connected with love and relationships. Are you madly in love? Longing to rush into living together, marriage and children? Or are you further down the line and moving very quickly into lifestyle changes which affect both of you? If you are speeding ahead in the relationship, or you recognize that rushing into things is your tendency, devote today to thinking about slowing down and discovering the benefits this brings.

The consequences of haste in a relationship can be immense – and often negative. More mistakes are made when we rush into decisions and there is less time to deal with any effects or feelings that arise. Most importantly, take time when deciding to marry. There is no need to rush into it if you are going to stay together, is there? The divorce courts are full of couples who say: 'We went into it too fast and then found we didn't know one another and were too different.' Few people say: 'We went into it too slowly, we were just too thoughtful and careful, and we took too long to get to know one another.' Committing to another person for life is the most exciting and challenging decision you will ever take, so be as sure as you can that it is the right one for both of you.

Don't commit if you want to:

- Change anything significant about your partner. It is very hard to make someone stop drinking/like your friends/want a baby or anything else, and it will put a great strain on the marriage.
- Escape from another situation – in order to get away from overprotective parents or another unhappy relationship, for example. Instead, move into a marriage from a clear, secure, happy space.
- Get to know your partner better. If you don't already know them very, very well, it's not time to commit.
- Solve a problem, such as dodgy finances or fear of being left on the shelf.
- Stop the nagging. Never agree to marry just to shut your partner (or anyone else) up, and don't agree just to please them – it is rarely wise in the long run.

The time to commit is when:

- You know your partner inside out, bad habits and all, and still adore him.
- You trust him completely and are sure he will be faithful and reliable.
- You can take the decision independently of anyone else's input.
- You have dealt with any major problems. Some little ones are bound to remain, but the big ones – such as excessive drinking or infidelity, lifestyle differences or whether to have children or not – need to be resolved.

Follow the same general 'don't rush' rules for any major aspect of your lives together, and it's wise to apply them to the small things in life as well. Live in haste, racing from one thing to another, and you'll find stress is overwhelming the relationship.

Take your time to make sure that your decisions are right for you

Day Twenty-Five

HAPPINESS

Today, simply be happy. Not when, if or because, but right now, just for its own sake. Too often we rely on the other person in our relationship to make us feel happy or we wait for happiness to come along, like a bus, and solve everything. We may believe that once all our problems are solved (though they never are), we'll feel happy. If you find yourself saying: 'We'd be happy if ...' or 'If he'd just ... I'd be so happy,' give it up right now! Whatever is stopping you from being happy, refuse to let it. Happiness is a state of mind and nothing will ever make you more happy than simply deciding to be so. Take the active decision to be responsible for your own happiness and to choose it over unhappiness on a daily basis.

How to stay happy in a relationship

Think happy thoughts

This requires a conscious effort on your part to choose thoughts that make you feel good and to combat unhappy, negative thoughts. Inner thoughts are like living beings, powerful, active and influential, so think carefully about which ones you allow in.

Nurture good feelings for your partner

Make this a priority. Relationships begin with a lot of warmth and love. If there is less now, then aim to raise the level by concentrating on positive feelings and behaving in a warm and loving way. When you feel warmth for your partner, your relationship feels good.

Be cautious of low moods

When you are feeling down and miserable, you may begin to pick holes in everything in your life and nothing will seem right or good enough. Resist this: simply comfort yourself or ask your partner for comfort, and wait for the mood to pass.

Remember that your life is your choice

And so is how you react to whatever comes. Try not to let things get the better of you. Instead, take charge of life. If you don't like the choices you've made, change them. If troubles strike, know that you will survive them, on your own or with others' support.

Repeat a positive mantra to yourself

Start every day by saying: 'Today I am willing to allow happiness into my life. I welcome it with open arms. I choose to be happy.'

Don't dwell on problems and setbacks

Take downturns as lightly as possible, don't let them trigger arguments and actively look for a solution to every problem.

To be happy in a relationship you need to cultivate happiness in yourself. Hold on tightly to the knowledge that you have a choice. Why be miserable when you can choose to be happy?

Let happiness be a way of living and loving

Day Twenty-Six

ACCEPTANCE

A big part of settling into a long-term relationship is accepting the other person. There will always be changes you want to make, aspects of the person that bother or irritate you, or habits you don't like or don't understand. Acknowledge that you are never going to like everything about your partner all of the time. Liking most things most of the time is doing pretty well. Accept those things you dislike in your partner (within reason) and let them go.

Focusing too much attention on the aspects you don't like will inevitably cause problems. An unimportant habit that irritates you – such as biting his nails, phoning his mother every day or leaving his clothes on the floor – can escalate into a reason to hate him if you let it. Any other feelings of discontent, resentment and anger you have will feed the irritation about your partner's habit until it becomes overwhelming.

Why do we find it so hard to accept someone just as they are? Partly because we enter a relationship with certain expectations, then try to get the person we've chosen to fit those expectations. Instead of waiting patiently, with genuine curiosity, to find out who they are, we look for signs that they will fit the ready-made mould we've already designed.

Keys to acceptance
Accept that you can't change another person
If he wants to change, you can certainly help him, but trying to change someone who isn't interested in changing will leave you frustrated, let down and helpless. Sometimes asking the person, kindly and specifically, to change a particular behaviour or habit works if he has the goodwill to do it, but that's as far as changing someone else can go.

Recognize that the only person you can change is yourself
Usually when we transform ourselves in some way, other people change their response to us. So if you want your partner to stop treating you like a doormat, stop behaving like one. If you want less arguing in the relationship, take responsibility for your side of the rows and stop. If you want your partner to open up and talk to you, tell him about your own feelings and be willing to really listen to his.

Focus on the positive

Concentrate on all you love about your partner and decide that you can live with a few irritating habits.

Take the focus off the source of irritation

Try laughing about it and telling yourself: 'Oh, well, so what if he leaves the bathroom in a mess/is always losing his car keys, it doesn't matter.'

Learning acceptance frees you to set out on the path to real relationship wisdom. Remember that no one is perfect, and that both our faults and our lovable qualities make us the unique individuals we are.

Acceptance is the key to peace and harmony

Day Twenty-Seven

RESOLVING CONFLICT: THE SOFTLY, SOFTLY APPROACH

Sometimes there are painful and difficult issues in a relationship which need to be discussed and sorted out, or problems that need solving. When something is troubling you or wrong in the relationship, one of you is probably going to bring it up at some stage, and the way in which you do this is crucial. All too often, the woman is the one who raises issues in relationships. It is a recognized fact that men are more fearful of discussing tensions and that women are better able to confront and deal with them. These gender-specific traits stem from evolutionary patterns, so it's best to work with, rather than resent, them.

How to raise issues in a way that leads to resolution rather than conflict:

Begin softly

Launching with a full-scale attack or an aggressive manner will switch your partner into defence mode and get you nowhere, so begin by appreciating your partner. For example, suppose the issue is that he is too distant and won't talk about his feelings. Begin by thanking him for his willingness to talk right now and to listen to what you have to say. Reaffirm your love and express how happy you are with him.

Talk about the problem using 'I' statements

Sentences that focus on your feelings, such as 'I feel frustrated and shut out when you won't talk to me about how you feel,' are easier for your partner to listen to and accept, and they avoid casting blame in his direction.

Tell your partner what you would like

Be as specific as possible. For example, say: 'I'd really like to know how you feel about us and whether you are happy with the way the relationship is going.'

Keep the mood light

If the conversation get tricky, introduce humour and keep the tone affectionate.

Stop sooner rather than later

Even if you get a good response, don't push on to deal with ten other issues that have been causing conflict. Stop, give your partner a hug and get on with something else.

If your partner stonewalls – that is, he refuses to respond or even disappears (for instance, behind a newspaper or computer) – STOP. This means your partner is feeling overwhelmed. Stonewalling is a stress response; it doesn't mean that he doesn't love you, but simply that he can't cope with the amount of information/ emotion/volume coming his way. What may feel normal to you could feel huge to your partner. If you follow, badger or insist, he will disappear further for longer. So back off and wait for another time, then make your approach soft, warm and brief. Your partner will only respond when he feels safe and can actually listen to you without feeling, rightly or wrongly, that he is being ambushed.

Tread softly, and solve difficult issues successfully

Day Twenty-Eight

NURTURING

To work successfully, a relationship needs nurturing. Just like a plant, it will grow stronger and thrive if it is treated with tenderness, fed and given the best possible advantages. In the early stages nurturing the relationship is easy. You are in love, the relationship is the centre of your life and there are few other demands. Later on other responsibilities can get in the way of nurturing it. Stress, exhaustion, work, children, health problems and financial pressures can all become major preoccupations.

Many divorced couples failed to nurture their relationship and then found that it had died. Often they realize, too late, that they didn't want to part and that there was so much to value in what they had together. When the relationship is in crisis, suddenly it becomes important again, and all other issues in life take a back seat. But by then it is so often too late: both partners are floundering and lost, with no idea of how to rekindle love and forge a new, even stronger union.

With love and effort, it is always possible to draw back from the brink. However, it is far better never to reach this point, and the way to ensure this is through nurturing.

How to nurture your partner

Keep romance alive
In the early days, being romantic is easy, but later on it takes a little extra thought and effort. No matter how busy you are, make time to write a romantic note and leave it for your partner to find, or to buy a little gift or to plan a candlelit dinner.

Never take each other for granted
Couples become so used to one another that they can stop noticing little details. Look at your partner with fresh eyes, listen to what he says and notice the small changes. Has your partner put on a little weight, changed what he wears, begun frowning with worry more often? If you don't notice what's going on, you can't respond to it.

Make room for surprises
Life's day-to-day routine becomes dull and predictable, and that is why surprises are so wonderful. Present your partner with a weekend away, a special night out or a thoughtful gift.

Treasure the special parts of the relationship
At the beginning all couples have special activities that they enjoy sharing, but as time goes by these 'luxuries' often disappear. Whatever your special things are – lingering baths together, passionate (not routine) sex, going for a walk or just talking – hang on to them (or enjoy finding new ones) and treat them as essential.

Be kind to each other
When one of you is sick, exhausted, disappointed, upset or feeling a failure, the other needs to be at his or her most sensitive and kind. Nurture your partner in whatever way he would most appreciate. Let him know that whatever goes on in the world outside, you will always love him just as much as before.

Remember that in order to nurture the relationship you need to nurture yourself, too, otherwise you will feel that you have nothing to give.

Nurture the love you share and watch it thrive

Day Twenty-Nine

TREASURE WHAT YOU HAVE

Concentrate on feeling lucky – it's the best feeling in the world, so enjoy it! Switching your mindset from unlucky or down to lucky can be hard at times, but the effort it well worth it. The ability to treasure what you have in a relationship, and everything connected with it, is a wonderful gift and one that we all have. All it takes is a little willingness.

Often we focus on what is missing in our lives, and this applies to relationships, too. What are you unhappy or discontent about at the moment? What do you wish you had or want to change? Do you wish you had more money, that your partner would change in some way, that life were easier, better, simpler? Do you want to live somewhere else or be slimmer, sexier or funnier? Concentrating on what is missing or wrong is draining and requires a lot of energy, which could be far better used elsewhere. It often makes you ill and damages the relationship. It also gives the world the message that you feel discontent, and this will be fed back to you by the people around you. Remember that what you give out, you will attract. Make the decision today to be lucky and to treasure what you have.

How to treasure your relationship

Act happy

Smile, whether you feel like it or not, at everyone you meet and even smile when you're alone. It will convince your brain that you're happy, and then you will start to feel happy. Remember that feelings follow behaviour; behave as though you feel great and you will. Sing, dance, laugh and enjoy life.

See abundance everywhere

Your life is filled with love, successes and things to feel good about. Start to notice them.

Measure your progress

Give thanks for the ways in which you've both grown and adapted, and all that you've learnt together. A relationship makes you wiser.

Value your health

Studies have proved that couples in long-term relationships are generally healthier than single people, so glow with vigour and feel content.

Cultivate an attitude of gratitude

Give thanks for all you have. In bed at night, go over all the good things that have happened throughout the day.

Appreciate your partner

Think about his good qualities, talents and abilities, and see him as unique and special. Take delight in the fact that he has chosen to be with you and that you were wise enough to choose him.

Treasuring what you have is simply a new habit to learn. Like any habit, it requires repetition before you can do it without thinking. The same applies to feeling lucky. For the next two weeks, walk around telling yourself you are lucky and you can be certain that, before long, people will be saying: 'You're so lucky, how do you do it?'

**Treasure what you have, and attract
more good luck into your life**

Day Thirty

CELEBRATE!

So, you've made it this far. Well done! Hopefully by now you are feeling optimistic about your relationship and the future. Whatever point you were at when you started this book, you should now be feeling better, stronger and more confident. Being in a relationship is one of life's richest blessings, and, if you love someone, there is nothing you can't resolve together. Working on the points raised in this book is way of investing in the relationship and acknowledging how important it is – that it's well worth the effort, time and trouble – and that's something to celebrate.

Congratulate yourself on getting this far and being willing to work on the relationship. Celebrate being with someone you care about so much and all the advances you've made. If you don't want to tell your partner exactly what the occasion is you're marking, simply say that you are rejoicing being with him, and that's cause enough.

Ways to celebrate your relationship:

- Do something different together or something familiar in a different setting – sex in the middle of the day, a picnic in the middle of the night or dinner in bed.
- Share a treat – perhaps a cake and a cup of coffee, or champagne and caviar.
- Have a night out enjoying a passionate opera, a romantic dinner or a sexy movie.
- Give each other a head-to-toe massage, with sensual aromatherapy oils and scented candles.
- Share a candlelit bath with bubbles, music and champagne.
- Cook dinner together, indulging in your favourite foods and plenty of legendary aphrodisiacs such as oysters and chocolate.
- Take a day off work just to be together.
- Shower your partner with romance – a sentimental card, a sexy present (and one for you), an early night . . .
- Surprise your partner – by kissing and making up sooner than usual after a fight, by giving in or by telling him that life's too short to argue.
- Take his breath away by paying special attention to the way you look.

Make this celebration the first of many, and don't limit yourself to just one from the above list – try them all! Celebrate every milestone you pass, no matter how small, making this a key feature of your journey through life together.

Celebrate the pure joy of being together

A FINAL WORD

Whatever you do in life is worth doing to the absolute best of your ability, including being in a relationship. Why settle for ordinary, mundane, okay, passable, middling or bearable when you can have extraordinary, wonderful, exciting, satisfying, passionate and fabulous – the kind of relationship you deserve? The choice is yours, and you make it every single day that you stay in a relationship. Promise yourself each day that, if you decide to stay with this person, you will actively choose to have a marvellous life with your partner and to make the relationship as good as it can be.

Preventing the negative from overwhelming the positive will help the relationship become a balanced and fulfilling one that will last. Keep this in mind, always, and let it be your guide when making decisions. Resolve to limit conflict and pain and to nurture all that is good between you. Choose to notice and appreciate your partner, and opt for love and peace over hurt and fights. Enjoy to the full the fruits of your choices – greater love, peace and harmony.

Resources

FURTHER READING

Biddulph, Steve and Shaaron, **How Love Works**, London, HarperCollins, 2000

Clephane, Ellen, **Dance of Love: What Fifty Couples Say Makes Successful Relationships Really Work**, Shaftesbury, Dorset, Element, 1996

Cole, Julia, **Make Love Work for You**, London, Hodder & Stoughton, 2000

Cornfield, Jack, and Hansen, Mark Victor, **Chicken Soup for the Couple's Soul**, London, Vermilion, 2000

Gottman, John, and Silver, Nan, **The Seven Principles for Making Marriage Work**, London, Orion Books, 2000

Gray, John, **Mars and Venus in Love**, London, Vermilion, 1996

Hayman, Suzie, **Make Your Honeymoon Last**, London, Hodder & Stoughton, 2000

Hendrix, Harville, **Getting the Love You Want: A Guide for Couples**, New York, NY, Henry Holt & Co., 2001

McGraw, Phillip C, **Relationship Rescue**, London, Vermilion, 2000

Quilliam, Susan, **Love Coach**, London, HarperCollins, 2000

Quilliam, Susan, **The Relate Guide to Staying Together**, London, Vermilion, 2001

Temsi, Carolyn, and Handley, Caro, **Love Wisdom**, New York, NY, Pocket Books, 1999